# BASS ALONG

## 10 FUNK AND SOUL MUSIC SONGS
### JAMES BROWN, TINA TURNER, BILL WITHERS and more

**Bass Along – 10 Funk And Soul Music Songs**

Copyright © 2013 by Bosworth Music GmbH

Covergestaltung: Knut Schötteldreier/Tim Field

BOE7704
ISBN 978-3-86543-798-3

Printed in the EU.

www.bosworth.de

## INHALT / CONTENTS

## INTRODUCTION

Playing the bass in a rock- or popband is the dream of many a young bassplayer. This book aims at getting you there! The bassplayer is the person who gives basic harmony and groove to a band; in order to aquire the necessary skills you should practise frequently in a band context, if possible. But how is it done without a band? What is important as a bassplayer?

The bass-grooves in this book are written as so-called "lead sheets" – you'll learn more about that on the next pages.This book doesn't require you to learn the original bass-lines note-by-note. This would confront you with lots and lots of written material and a tedious learning process. What's more, I want to offer an easy method by which you as a beginner can start playing along with your favourite rock- and popsongs in next to no time and in the style of the originals!

The additional CD features the songs from this book, recorded with voice, guitar, keyboards and drums. Furthermore, there is a version of each song without bass, enabling you to play along as you would in a real band.

We wish you lots of fun while practising and even more success as a bassplayer!

## VORWORT

Bass in einer Rock- oder Popband zu spielen ist der Traum vieler junger Bassisten/-innen. Und auf dem Weg zu diesem Ziel soll dieses Buch behilflich sein. Als Bassist in einer Band ist man vor allem für den Groove und das harmonische Fundament zuständig. Dazu ist neben instrumentalspezifischen Techniken und Notenkenntnissen vor allem auch viel Üben notwendig. Wie soll man aber ohne Gitarre, Drums und Keyboard das Spielen in einer Band üben? Worauf kommt es als Bassist besonders an?

Die Bass-Grooves sind in diesem Buch als sogenannte „Lead-sheets" notiert, dazu erfährst du auf den kommenden Seiten noch mehr. Es ist nicht die Idee dieses Buches, die Basslinien der Originalaufnahmen Ton für Ton wiederzugeben und zu üben. Dafür bräuchtest du seitenweise Noten, die du Takt für Takt üben müsstest. Es soll vielmehr eine übersichtliche Methode erarbeitet werden, bereits als Anfänger mit einfachen Mitteln berühmte Rocksongs, die jeder aus Radio und Fernsehen kennt, stilecht und angelehnt an das Original mitzuspielen.

Auf der beiliegenden CD sind die Lieder aus diesem Buch mit Gesang, Gitarre, Keyboard und Schlagzeug aufgenommen. Außerdem ist zu jedem Lied auch eine Version ohne Bass aufgenommen, damit du wie in einer echten Band als Bassist mitspielen kannst.

Wir wünschen dir viel Spaß beim Üben und viel Erfolg auf deinem Weg zum Rock- oder Popbassisten.

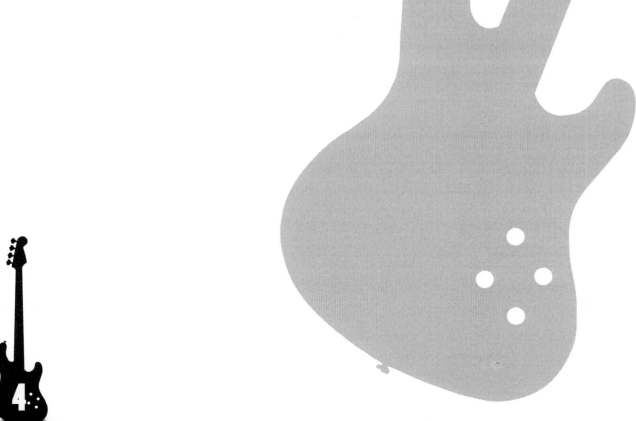

## EXPLANATION OF THE LEAD SHEETS

Rock songs consist of different parts, which are usually repeated several times during a song. The most important parts are "verse" and "chorus", as well as there are "intro", "outro" and instrumental solo parts. "Bridge" is the name for a part which connects to more important parts where there is a vocal line in the original, an "interlude" divides parts without a vocal line; if there is a very significant instrumental line in an interlude it is called "riff".

The rocksongs are organized on so-called "lead-sheets", whereby the notation in this book is a little different from what you might have seen in other books. Normally, you will find page after page of written music, on which every minute change or variation of groove is painstakingly notated. These aren't lead-sheets, but would rather be refered to as "transcriptions". Lead-sheets actually focus on the truly important parameters, thereby omitting any superfluos variations or passing notes.
The goal is to quickly get an idea of what the whole song is about and get a firm grip on the groove.

This brings us to another big difference in relation to normal notation, where the visual aspect of the written material very often dominates the logical aspect of a song's form; one very important aspect is keeping an equal distance between notes, which subsequently determines the line breaks, and very often you'll find that the form of a song is completely irrelevant in this process – the verse or chorus of a song starts in the middle of a stave or there might be a varying number of bars in each stave. This makes it very difficult to find the beginning or end of a part of the song, but exactly this is very important when playing in a band. In that sense, we want to make things as easy as possible for you.

In this book, everything is written according to the form of the song. When looking at the music, you'll see that almost every system has 4 bars. Pop- and rockmusic is mostly symmetrical, meaning that songparts mostly have 4, 8 or 16 bars. In some songs the form varies by an additional 2 bars, for example. Very seldom, you'll find irregular forms (1, 3, or 5 bars).

Since the songs mostly have a symmetrical form (e.g.: intro 4 bars, verse 8 bars, chorus 8 bars etc.), melodies and grooves are repeated accordingly. So one other great advantage of this notation is that you'll immediately recognize grooves that are repeated, because they are written next to each other. This makes things much easier while reading the music, and helps you to memorize the song much faster.

## ERKLÄRUNG DER SONGABLÄUFE

Rocksongs bestehen aus unterschiedlichen Teilen, die im Laufe eines Songs immer wiederkehren. Die wichtigsten beiden sind die Strophe (engl. „Verse") und der Refrain (engl. „Chorus"). Dazu kommen ggf. Einleitung und Schlussteil (engl. „Intro" und „Outro"), Soli der verschiedenen Instrumente und Überleitungsteile. Überleitungsteile mit Gesang nennt man „Bridge", Überleitungsteile ohne Gesang entweder „Interlude" oder, wenn sie besonders markante Instrumentalbegleitungen haben, „Riff".

Die Rocksongs sind als sogenannte Ablaufpläne (engl. „lead-sheets") notiert. Allerdings unterscheidet sich die Notation in diesem Buch etwas zu der normalen Notation, die du vielleicht aus anderen Büchern gewohnt bist. Normalerweise findet man in Songbooks oft seitenlange Noten, in denen jede kleine Variation des Grooves (oder der Melodie) ausnotiert wurde. Das sind eigentlich keine Leadsheets im engeren Sinn, sondern man würde sie eher als Transkription (eine detailgenaue Notation) bezeichnen. Leadsheets konzentrieren sich dagegen auf das Wesentliche und Variationen oder irgendwelche Durchgangsnoten brauchen nicht notiert zu werden.
Das Ziel ist es, dass man schnell einen Überblick über die Form des Stückes bekommt und die Grooves auf einen Blick erfassen kann.

Hier kommen wir zu einem weiteren wichtigen Unterschied zu einer herkömmlichen Notation. Noten werden fast immer unter dem Gesichtspunkt des Notensatzes aufgeschrieben. Man versucht ein möglichst ausgewogenes Notenbild zu erstellen, d.h. die Abstände zwischen den einzelnen Noten werden berechnet und nach ihnen richten sich alle Zeilenumbrüche. Dabei wird allerdings die Form des Songs überhaupt nicht beachtet, oft fangen Strophen oder Refrains mitten in der Notenzeile an, es gibt unterschiedlich viele Takte pro Zeile, was es schwierig macht, Anfang und Ende eines Songteils zu finden. Dabei ist es gerade in einer Band enorm wichtig, die Form des Songs genau zu kennen.

In diesem Buch haben wir alle Noten der Form des Stückes entsprechend notiert. Wenn du die Noten anschaust, wirst du schnell bemerken, dass fast alle Notenzeilen 4 Takte haben.
Pop- und Rocksongs sind eigentlich immer symmetrisch aufgebaut, d.h. ein Formteil hat 4, 8 oder 16 Takte, je nachdem. In manchen Stücken weicht die Form etwas ab und es werden ab und an 2 Takte eingeschoben. Ganz selten gibt es ungerade Formen (z.B. 1, 3 oder 5 Takte).

Da Songs fast immer in dieser symmetrischen Form (z.B. Intro 4 Takte, Strophe 8 Takte, Refrain 8 Takte etc.) komponiert sind, wiederholen sich natürlich auch Melodien oder Grooves der Form entsprechend. Deshalb ist ein weiterer großer Vorteil dieser Art der Notation, dass man sehr schnell sieht, wann sich Grooves wiederholen, da sie jetzt direkt übereinanderstehen. Der Effekt ist, dass man den Song wesentlich schneller auswendig spielen kann und die Noten nur noch als Unterstützung braucht.

Lots of songs end with „repeat and fade out". Repeat the last pattern of the song as long as you can still hear the other instruments playing and try to play softer and softer as you go along.

All of this sounds very sophisticated, but if you simply read the lead sheets while listening to the music, you will find out that it is quite easy. The song parts of the recordings on the CD are absolutely identical to the parts of the original songs. I warmly recommend listening to the original recordings, while reading the lead sheets. This will give you an idea of the style and sound of the original music.
Because we recorded all the songs with voice, we had to adapt the keys to the tonal range of the singer every now and again.

## TAB NOTATION

In TAB, we've also changed things a bit: normally, TAB and notes are written directly on top of each other, thus enabling a quick reference for positioning.
The disadvantage of this concept lies in having to use lots of pages to write down a complete song, thus causing you to turn pages a lot and distracting you from playing. That's why we separated TAB from the written music and put it on a separate lead sheet.
Subsequently, we were able to accomodate all songs onto a double page – no more turning pages while playing along!
If you're not firm with reading music yet, and sometimes tend to get stuck, you can allways refer to TAB while practising the groove-parts, thereby recognising another major advantage:
since you're immediately returning to the lead sheet after having consulted TAB, you'll memorize fingerings much faster than by constantly reading TAB.
At the end of the day, you should be able to play everything completely by heart and forget about the written music.

Oft enden die Lieder, indem der letzte Songteil immer wieder wiederholt und dabei ausgeblendet wird. Das nennt man „repeat and fade out". Wiederhole bei diesen Songs den letzten Teil solange, bis du die anderen Instrumente auf der Aufnahme nicht mehr hören kannst und versuche auch, immer leiser dabei zu werden.

Das klingt jetzt alles sehr theoretisch, aber wenn du die Leadsheets zur Musik mitliest, wirst du schnell entdecken, dass alles sehr einfach funktioniert. Die Abläufe auf der CD sind übrigens genauso wie im Original des entsprechenden Songs. Es ist sehr hilfreich, auch die Originalaufnahmen anzuhören und dabei das Leadsheet mitzulesen. Du bekommst so auch einen Eindruck von der Stilistik und der Stimmung des Songs.
Da wir alle Songs mit echtem Gesang aufgenommen haben, mussten wir ab und an Tonarten der Songs etwas ändern, um sie an den Stimmbereich des Sängers anzupassen.

## DIE TABULATUR

Noch ein Unterschied: Auch bei der Notation der TABs haben wir etwas geändert. Normalerweise stehen Noten und TAB direkt untereinander. Wenn man nicht weiß, wie man eine Note greift, schaut man auf die Tabulatur.
Der Nachteil ist, dass man wieder oft mehrere Notenseiten braucht, um einen kompletten Song zu notieren. D.h. es bleibt nicht aus, blättern zu müssen, was oft sehr nervig ist, da man mitten im Song anhalten oder ein paar Noten weglassen muss, um umzublättern. Aus diesem Grund haben wir die Tabulatur von den Noten abgekoppelt und in einem extra Leadsheet notiert.
Der große Vorteil ist, dass wir jetzt alle Songs auf jeweils einer Doppelseite notieren konnten, und man nicht mehr zu blättern braucht, wenn man zum Playback spielt.
Wenn du noch nicht so firm im Notenlesen bist und bei einigen Noten „hängen" bleibst, kannst du beim separaten Üben der einzelnen Groove-Parts umblättern und in der Tabulatur nachsehen, wie man die Note greift. Du wirst schnell merken, dass dies sogar noch einen Vorteil mit sich bringt:
Indem du nur kurz nachsiehst, wie man die Note greift, dann aber wieder ohne die TABs nur nach den Noten spielst, wirst du dir die Griffe viel schneller einprägen, als wenn du ständig auf die Tabulatur „spickst".
Und am Ende solltest du ganz ohne die Noten auskommen und den Song auswendig spielen.

## TIPS FOR PRACTISING

Start by practising all relevant grooves for a song without the CD at first, in order to make them your own 'flesh and blood'. If you have a teacher, let him play the different parts slowly for you.
Then you may slowly increase the tempo and finally play along with the playback. Go for the full version at first – it gives you the recorded bass for orientation. If that works fine, you can then try the playback-version.
Allways think of the bass as the basis of a song. Therefore it has to have a firm grip on the groove and basic harmony.

### Special suggestions for rehearsals in a band

Remember the following points when rehearsing with a band:

• Always start very slowly
• Rehearse every part of the song seperately.
• Give a lot of attention to the connections of song parts, e.g. play the last four bars of the verse and the first four bars of the following chorus directly afterwards. Repeat this several times.
• Make sure, which part to rehearse first and don't stop playing just because of one wrong note somewhere. Try to go on in case of minor mistakes.
• When you have worked out the song in slow tempo you can play it a little bit faster.
• Before performing the song on stage you should definitely have lots of run-throughs. Don't stop in any case, always try to go on. This is quite important, because on stage things will happen anyway. Mistakes are common in music, nobody's perfect! Even the big stars do make mistakes on stage – if they don't let you know, you will never find out.

## ÜBETIPPS

Beginne damit, zu jedem Song erst einmal alle vorkommenden Grooves sorgfältig ohne die Musik zu üben, bis diese in Fleisch und Blut übergehen. Wenn du Unterricht hast, kann dein Lehrer dir die verschiedenen Teile langsam vorspielen.
Dann kannst du langsam das Tempo erhöhen und schließlich zum Playback versuchen mitzuspielen. Nimm zuerst die Vollversion, so kannst du dich zunächst noch am eingespielten Bass orientieren. Wenn das gut klappt, versuch es zur Playback-Version.
Denk immer dran, dass der Bass das Fundament eines Songs ist. Er gibt die Grundtöne der Harmonien vor und muss deshalb besonders sicher und „Groove-fest" sein.

### Besondere Übetipps beim Proben mit der Band

Folgendes solltet ihr beachten, wenn ihr das Lied mit einer Band probt:

• Beginnt in einem langsamen Tempo.
• Probt auch jetzt erst jeden einzelnen Songteil getrennt.
• Probt besonders die Übergänge von einem Songteil zum nächsten, z.B. indem ihr die letzten vier Takte des ersten und die ersten vier Takte des nächsten Songteils übt und das ganze mit einer kurzen Pause dazwischen mehrmals wiederholt.
• Besprecht immer, bevor ihr spielt, welchen Abschnitt des Songs ihr spielen wollt und brecht nicht mittendrin ab, nur weil sich ein Mitspieler verspielt hat. Versucht bei kleinen Fehlern, trotzdem weiter zu spielen.
• Wenn ihr den Song gut erarbeitet habt, könnt ihr ein bisschen schneller spielen.
• Bevor ihr den Song auf der Bühne spielt, übt unbedingt ganz oft, das Stück ohne Unterbrechung vom Anfang bis zum Schluss durchlaufen zu lassen. Auch bei kleinen Fehlern unbedingt weiter spielen, die passieren auch im Konzert – übrigens nicht nur euch, sondern auch den großen Bands: Niemand ist fehlerfrei!

# GET DOWN ON IT

## KOOL & THE GANG

Words & Music by Ronald Bell, Eumir Deodato, Robert Mickens, James Taylor, Charles Smith, Robert Bell & George Brown

♩ = 110

**PICK UP**

**INTRO**

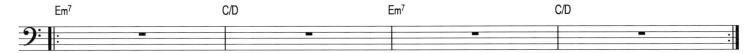

**CHORUS**

**VERSE**

# GET DOWN ON IT TAB

## PICK UP

## INTRO

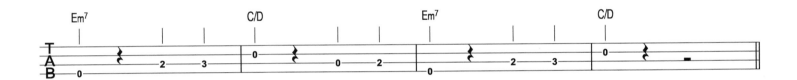

## CHORUS

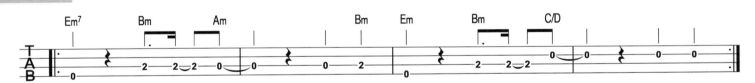

## VERSE

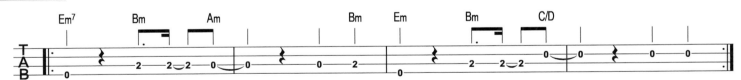

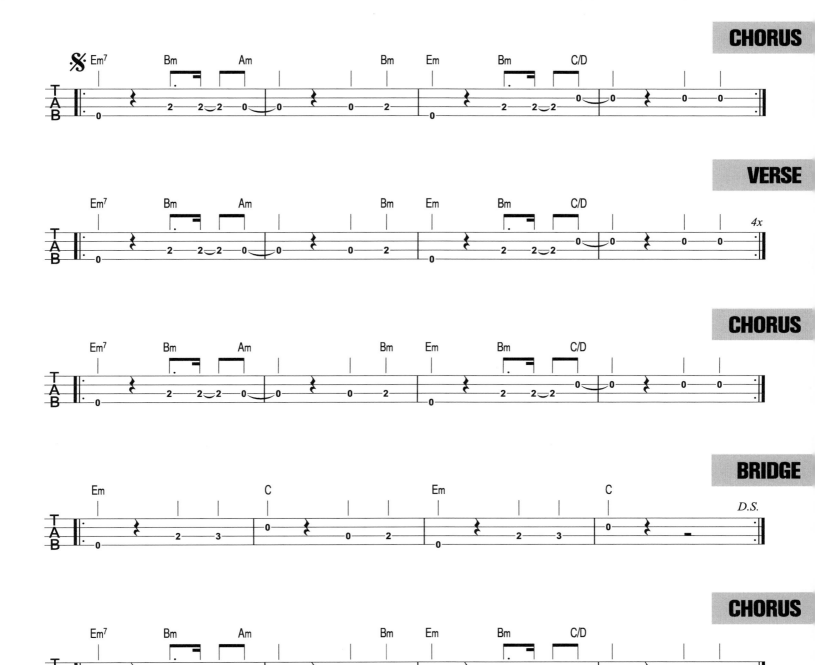

# WE DON'T NEED ANOTHER HERO

♩ = 98

## TINA TURNER

Words & Music by Terry Britten & Graham Lyle

**INTRO**

**VERSE**

**PRE-CHORUS**

*play this bar only 2. time*

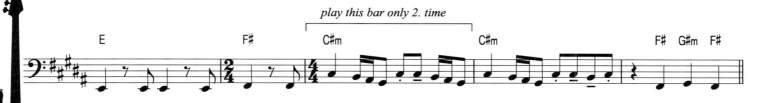

12

**CHORUS**

**BRIDGE**

**SAX SOLO**

**CHORUS**

# We Don't Need Another Hero TAB

## INTRO

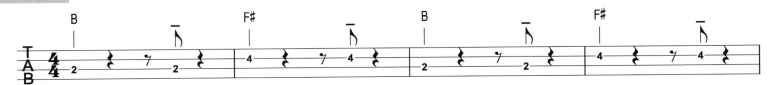

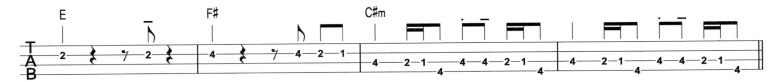

## VERSE

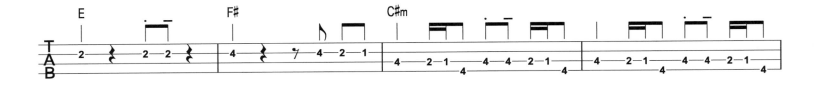

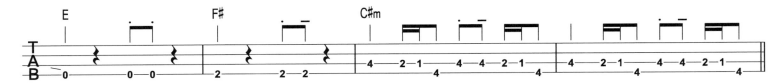

## PRE-CHORUS

*play this bar only 2. time*

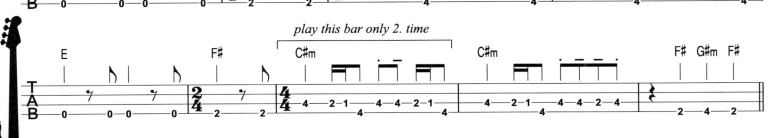

14

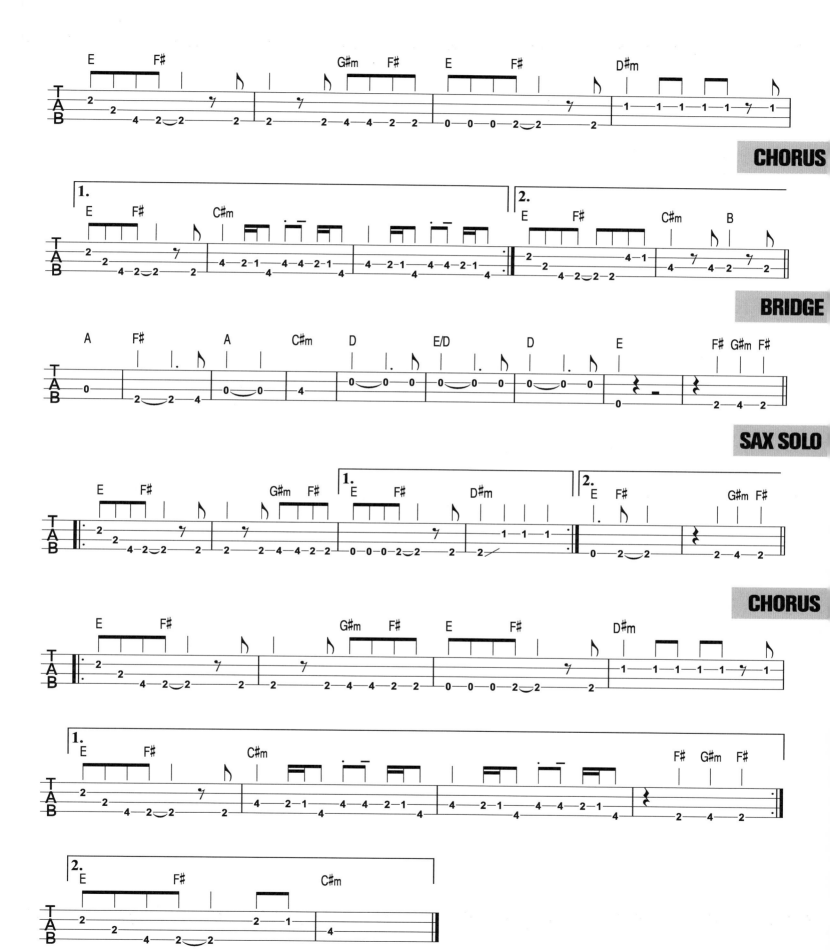

**CHORUS**

**BRIDGE**

**SAX SOLO**

**CHORUS**

# UNCHAIN MY HEART

## RAY CHARLES

Words & Music by Teddy Powell & Bobby Sharp

♩ = 152

SAX SOLO

OUTRO

# UNCHAIN MY HEART TAB

**INTRO**

**CHORUS**

**BRIDGE**

**CHORUS**

SAX SOLO

OUTRO

# YEAH RIGHT

## DIONNE BROMFIELD

Words & Music by Dionne Bromfield

♩ = 119

**INTRO**

**VERSE 1**

**CHORUS**

21

# YEAH RIGHT TAB

## INTRO

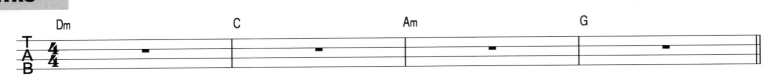

## VERSE 1

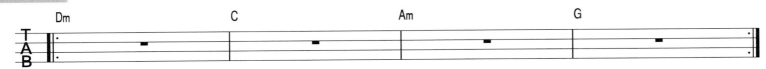

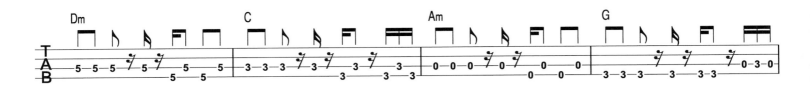

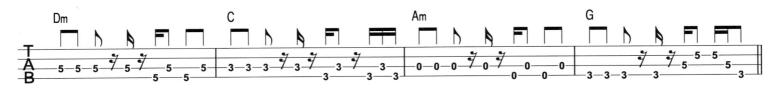

## CHORUS

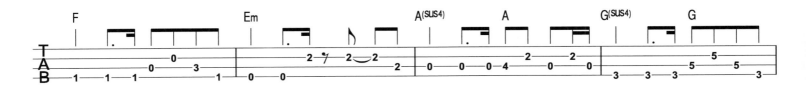

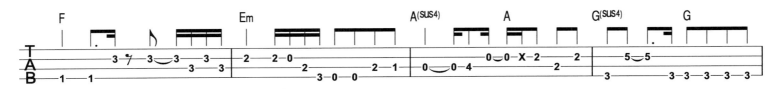

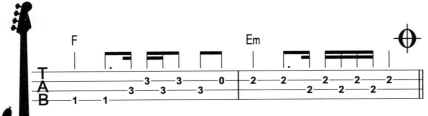

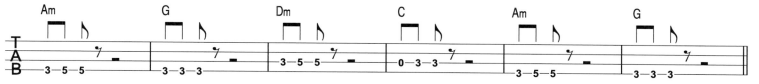

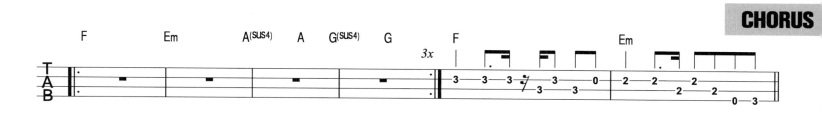
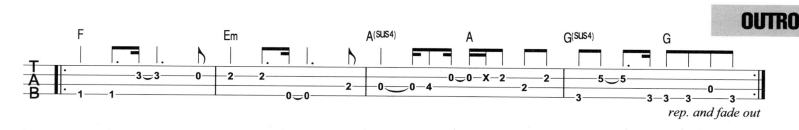

*rep. and fade out*

# AIN'T NO SUNSHINE

## BILL WITHERS

Words & Music by Bill Withers

♩ = 80

**CHORUS**

**BRIDGE**

**CHORUS**

# AIN'T NO SUNSHINE TAB

**CHORUS**

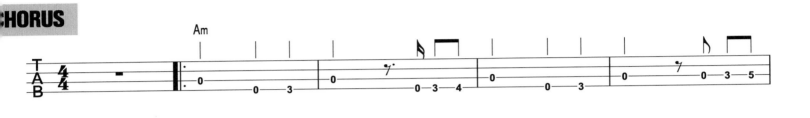

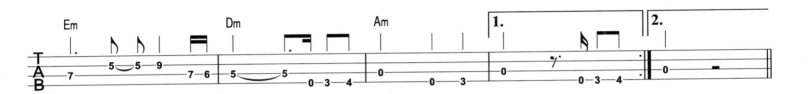

**BRIDGE**

**CHORUS**

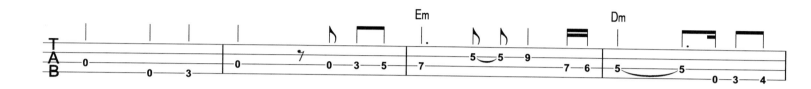

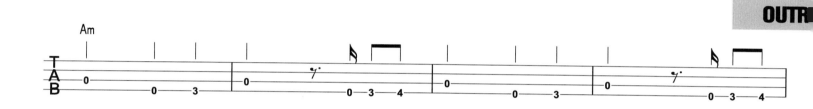

# SON OF A PREACHERMAN

## DUSTY SPRINGFIELD

Words & Music by John Hurley & Ronnie Wilkins

♩ = 90

**INTRO**

**VERSE**

**CHORUS**

**INTERL.**

**VERSE**

# SON OF A PREACHERMAN TAB

**INTRO**

**VERSE**

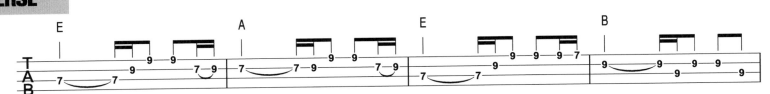

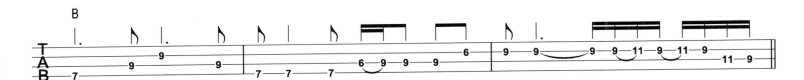

**CHORUS**

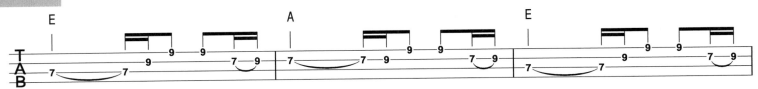

**INTERL.**

**VERSE**

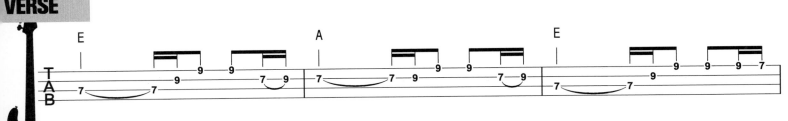

30.

# I SAY A LITTLE PRAYER

## ARETHA FRANKLIN

♩ = 133

Words by Hal David
Music by Burt Bacharach

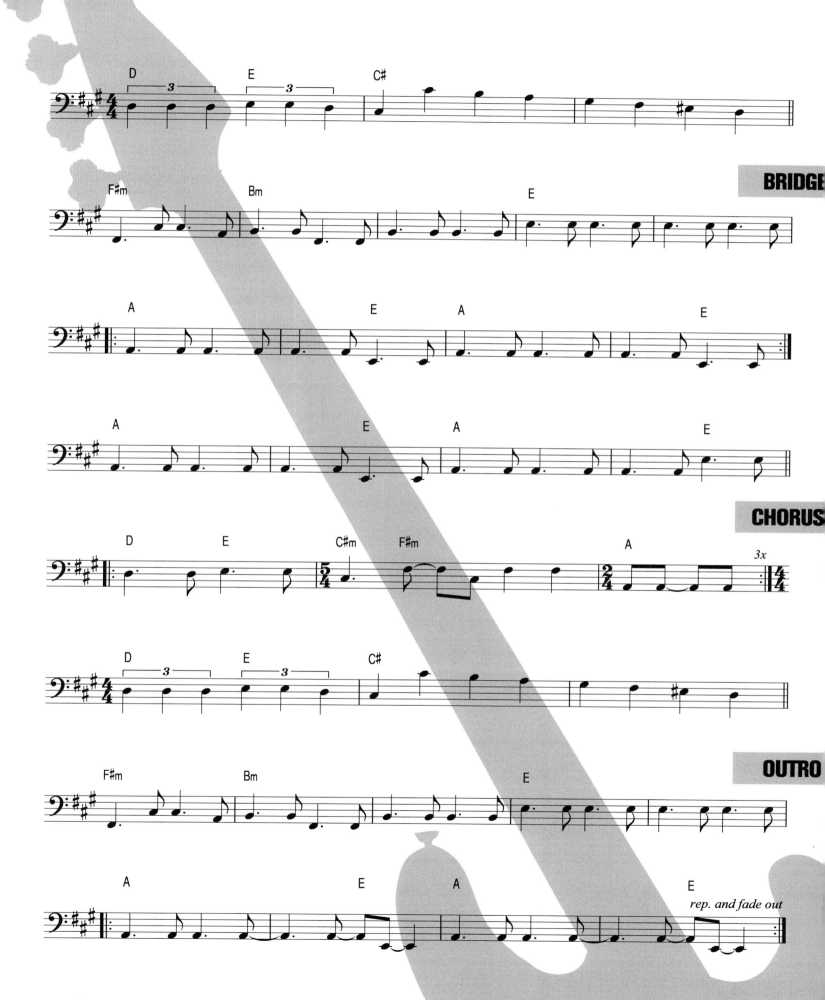

BRIDGE

CHORUS

OUTRO

# I SAY A LITTLE PRAYER TAB

## INTRO

## VERSE

## CHORUS

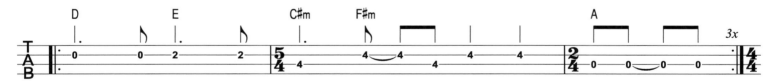

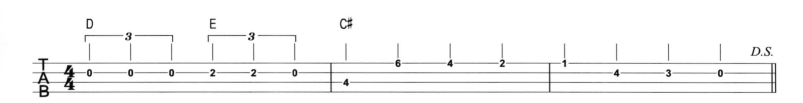

## CHORUS

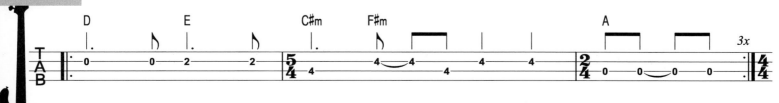

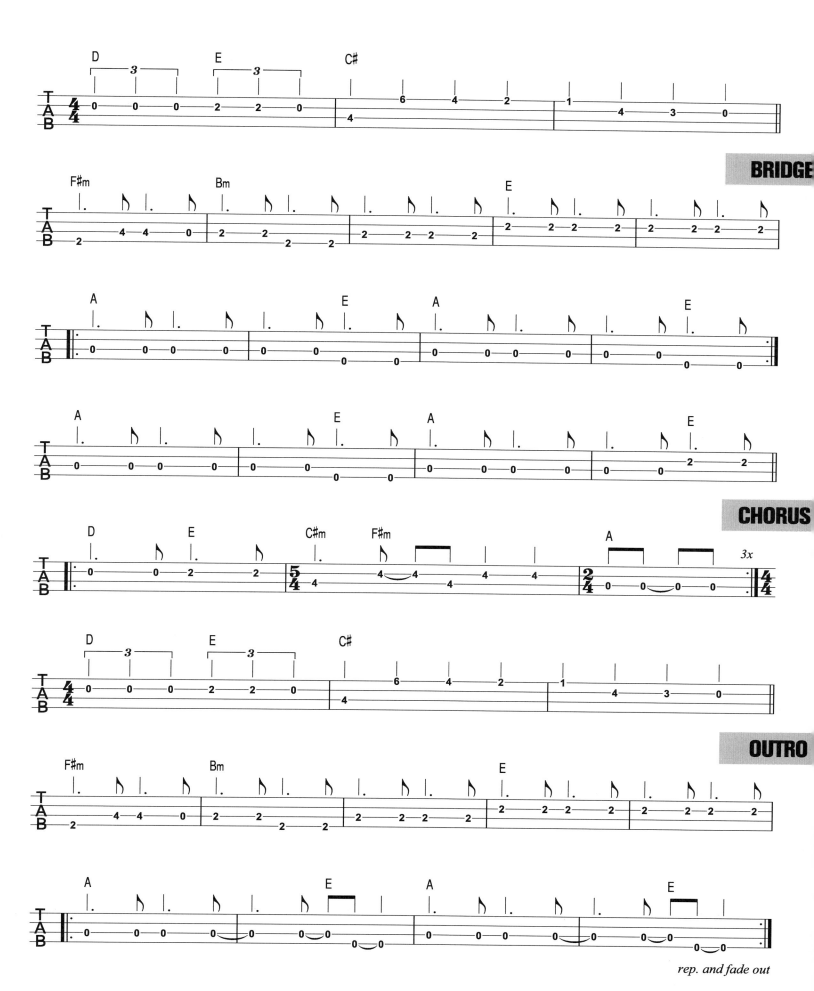

# LOVELY DAY
## BILL WITHERS

♩ = 98

Words & Music by Skip Scarborough & Bill Withers

**INTRO**

**VERSE**

# LOVELY DAY TAB

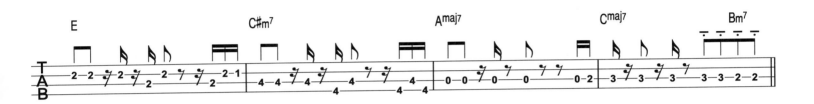

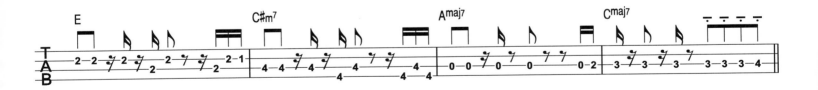

38

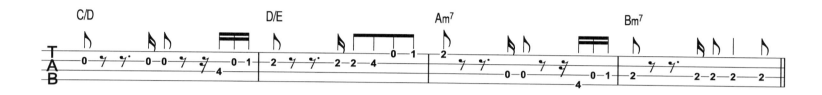

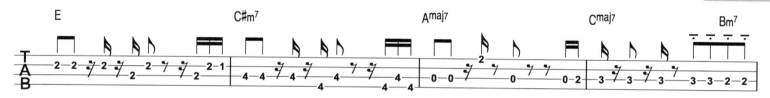

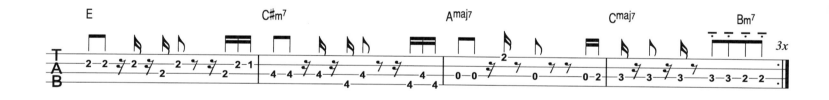

*rep. and fade out*

# Doo Wop (That Thing)

## LAURYN HILL

♩ = 100

Words & Music by Lauryn Hill

**INTRO**

**VERSE**

**BRIDGE**

**PRE-CHORUS**

**CHORUS**

# DOO WOP (THAT THING) TAB

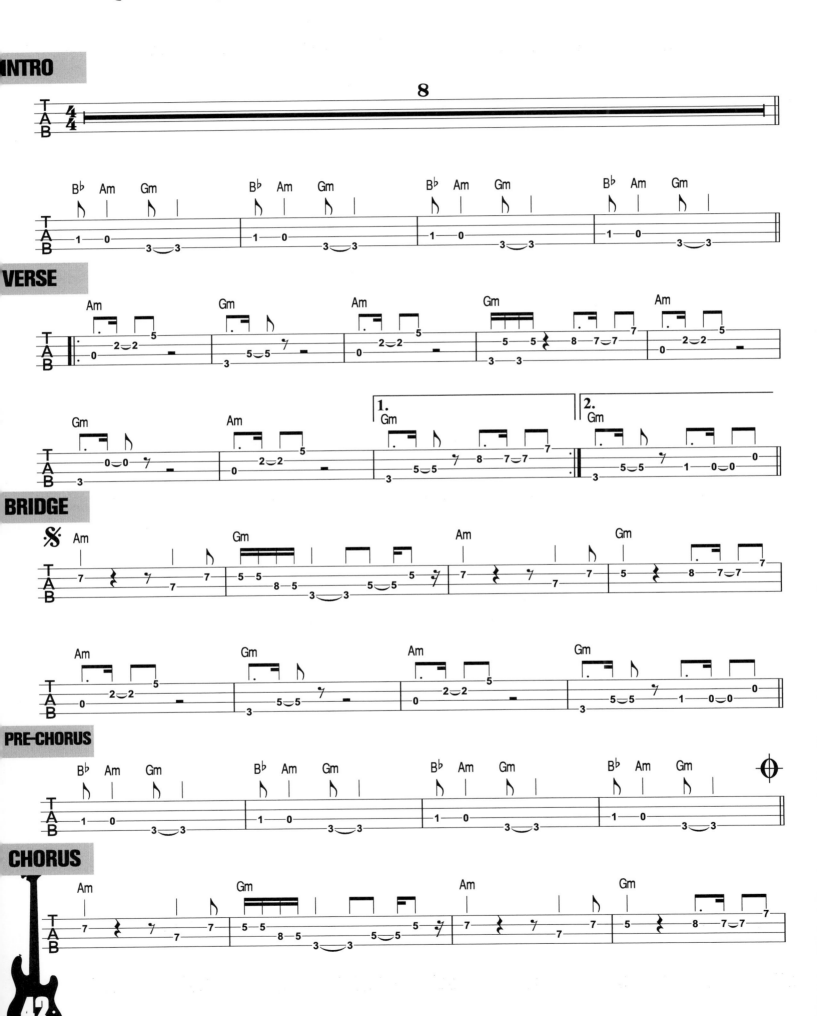

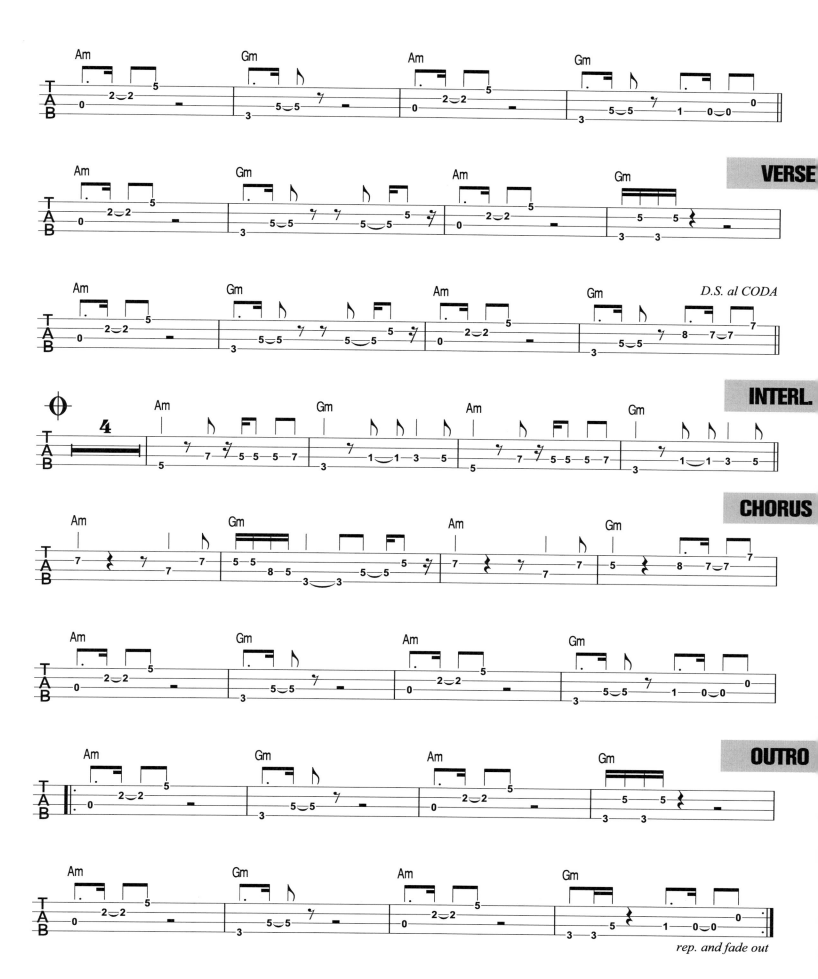

*rep. and fade out*

**43**

# GIVE IT UP OR TURN IT A LOOSE

♩ = 111

**JAMES BROWN**

Words & Music by Charles Bobbitt

## CHORUS

## BRIDGE

## CHORUS

44

G⁷

*4x*

Dm

*9x*

G⁷

*rep. ad lib. and fade out*

# GIVE IT UP OR TURN IT A LOOSE TAB

## CHORUS

## BRIDGE

## CHORUS

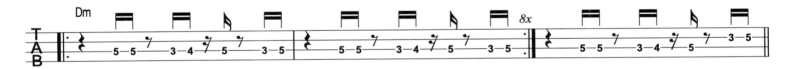

## BRIDGE

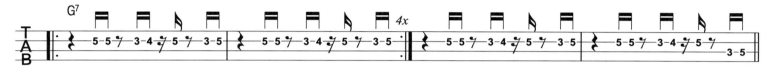

## CHORUS

## OUTRO

*rep. ad lib. and fade out*

# CD-Tracklisting